Cockermouth and District

IN OLD PHOTOGRAPHS

J. BERNARD BRADBURY

J. Bernard Bradbury

Alan Sutton Publishing Limited
Phoenix Mill · Far Thrupp · Stroud
Gloucestershire

First Published 1994

British Library Cataloguing in Publication Data.
A catalogue record for this book is available from the British Library.

ISBN 0-7509-0794-0

Typeset in 9/10 Sabon.
Typesetting and origination by
Alan Sutton Publishing Limited.
Printed in Great Britain by
Ebenezer Baylis, Worcester.

Main Street in more leisurely days, when the presence of a photographer was obviously an event.

Contents

Introduction 6

1. The Town From Above 11
2. Street Scenes 17
3. Shops and Prices 37
4. River Scenes 45
5. The Castle and other Homes 57
6. Churches and Schools 67
7. Industry 83
8. The Railway 99
9. Celebrations and Celebrities 107
10. Leisure Activities 115

Acknowledgements 128

Introduction

Cockermouth owes its existence to the river system. The nearby Roman camp of Derventio, modern Papcastle, was situated at the northern end of a crossing of the River Derwent, which flows from east to west just north of the present town centre. Here was an important road junction in the back-up to Hadrian's Wall. Also originating in the central Lakeland fells, the Cocker flows from the south to enter the Derwent here, hence the name of the town. At this confluence grew the Norman and medieval settlements, a natural administrative and trading centre for a number of converging valleys.

Little happened after the Romans left about AD 400 until the Normans arrived, but place names and Anglian remains in nearby churches prove the continued existence of communities in the area. Governing the district first from the former Roman site, the Normans soon moved to the present castle site on the end of a ridge between the rivers at their confluence. The town

The east end of All Saints church.

Cockermouth and District

IN OLD PHOTOGRAPHS

Looking down the River Cocker from Kirkbank.

This postcard was probably published early to mid-twentieth century. Of particular interest is the race which ran from the Ladyboat weir on the Derwent to power the High Gote and two Low Gote mills before rejoining the river. A sluice gate controlled the flow in the by-fall which can be seen returning unwanted water from the race to the Derwent. Brewery buildings screen the castle. The pre-1938 road bridge crosses the mouth of the Cocker. Are the frames on the extreme left tenter frames for Harris's linen mill which is off the picture to the left?

developed below the castle and for some distance west along the line of the present Main Street. In 1260 about 180 burgage properties were listed, in addition to the mills, workshops, etc. of an active and growing community. Excavations in 1980 proved habitation at the western end of Main Street by 1300.

Cockermouth developed as a typical medieval town, having a broad main street of burgesses' houses, each with a burgage plot stretching to the usual 'back lane' – the Derwent bank on the north and Back Lane (now South Street) on the south. This basic layout of streets and plots still largely remains, one reason for the town's inclusion as one of the fifty-one 'gem towns' selected in 1965 by the British Council for Archaeology as being worthy of special care in preservation and development, 'so splendid and so precious that ultimate responsibility for them should be a national concern'.

The town grew in importance as shown by the fact that at one time there were six MPs for the former county of Cumberland – two for Carlisle, two for Cockermouth and two for the county as a whole, and voting for these last two took place in Cockermouth! In addition to its market town life, it was

The crossing of the Cockermouth to Workington road, now demolished. Christ Church is in the background.

An elaborate commemorative arch erected on Cocker Bridge for the marriage of Prince Edward to Alexandra, 1863.

A Main Street crowd on fair day.

involved in West Cumberland trade. Although geographically cut off from much of the country it was linked to national events through the lords of the manor, the castle owners including the Lucy family (pre-1365); Percy, Earls of Northumberland (1385–1670); Seymour, Dukes of Somerset (1670–1750); and Wyndham (since 1750). Many of these were largely absentee landlords as far as Cockermouth was concerned, being involved in state affairs from one of their other, more accessible, seats.

Always a textile area, the town had a fulling mill by 1156, probably earlier. When machinery was invented to speed up spinning and weaving the domestic industry declined and Cockermouth, with its ample water supply, became a mill town. In the mid-nineteenth century there were over forty industrial sites – mills (wool, linen, cotton), hat factories, tanneries and smaller concerns making chairs, churns, mangle rollers, nails, farm machinery, etc. Throughout this period of industrial activity, now over, the town remained an important agricultural centre and today farming, tourism, one factory, a brewery and a growing number of small commercial and business concerns provide local employment, supplemented by industry along the West Cumbrian coastal belt, in particular Sellafield. Most mill buildings have been demolished, but some remain, converted to other uses.

The buildings of the town, past and present, have been well documented in a series of books of sketches under the general title 'Cockermouth in Pictures'. This book provides an opportunity to record people, street scenes, activities and events in the life of the town, although buildings are also included. Some references are made to the surrounding villages, which look to Cockermouth as their town centre.

Earlier this century, and still today, professional firms have produced postcard views – Raphael Tuck, Valentine, Francis Frith, etc. – but local photographers have also realized the value of their surroundings and recorded many street views. Of particular value are some one hundred magic lantern slides, the work of W.H. Youdale, a Cockermouth draper, showing the town in the 1890s. Unfortunately the records of the local press before 1975 were destroyed in a cellar flood. Today the record is continued by the town's Civic Trust and a number of enthusiastic individuals. The topics included in the following selection have been largely decided by the availability of photographs and by their quality.

A few photographs have been included which record recent events of historic interest in the life of the town, chiefly the opening of new community buildings – fire HQ, factory, clinic, scout centre, etc. A record of 1987 may not be an 'old photograph' in 1994, but it will become older every year!

J.B.B.

SECTION ONE

The Town From Above

An aerial photograph or a map can convey information which it would take many pages to describe and can indicate the position of features in the layout of the town impossible to show in any other way. In addition the majority of people enjoy seeing such a portrayal of a town, making armchair journeys of discovery. In this first section of the book five aerial views and maps have been reproduced, covering four centuries, with the twofold purpose of giving enjoyment and of providing quickly found reference when using the remainder of this volume.

Further aerial views are to be found on pp. 34 and 77.

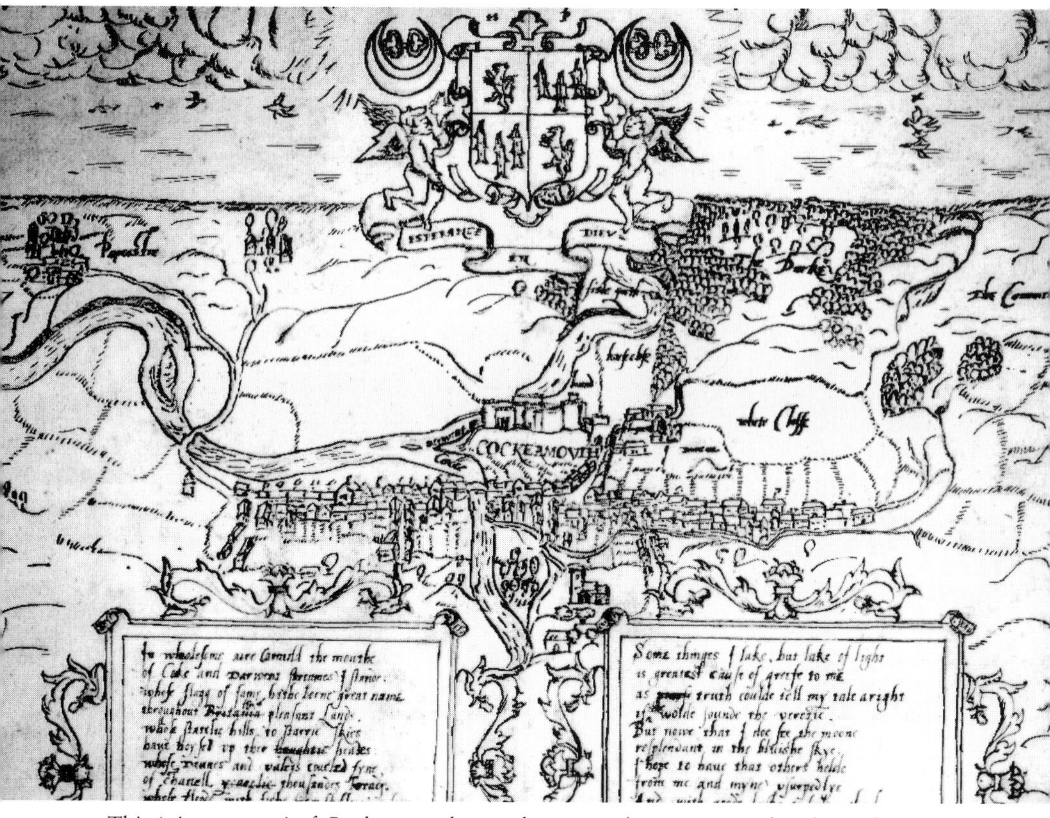

This 'picture map' of Cockermouth was drawn in about 1620 and is the earliest known. It shows clearly the river system and the medieval road pattern, little changed today. The 'Cocce' comes from the south to join the Derwent flowing east to west, with a rather fanciful castle at the confluence. Bitter Beck flows from the east into the Cocker.

Main Street (then Below Bridge) runs west to east and after crossing the river branches into Castlegate going up to Castle Garth and the castle and into Market Place leading east to St Helen's Street, the route in and out of the town on this side. Sullart Street/Gallowbarrow leads south at the western end of the town; nearer the river is Challoner Street and just before Castlegate little Market Street goes to a footbridge over the beck and then Church Steps and Church Walk lead to All Saints church. Further east Kirkgate goes south, crossing the beck by a ford and footbridge, then on to the Lorton Valley and Whinlatter Pass. These are modern street names – they varied over the centuries. The map clearly shows the built-up areas and the extent of the town at this time. The houses would be wattle and daub with thatched roofs.

The map is of interest for what is omitted as well as for what it shows. There were no streets to the north of Below Bridge, just an open river bank, and no Station Street to the south. Beyond the farm just east of the castle the road became a farm track. Gardens are shown and fields come close in to the town.

The coat of arms above the map includes the Percy lion and the three pike of the Lucy family (pike = luce). Maud, a Lucy, married Henry Percy, first Earl of Northumberland, in 1385. The Percy family were lords of the manor of Cockermouth from 1385 to 1670, which includes the date of this map.

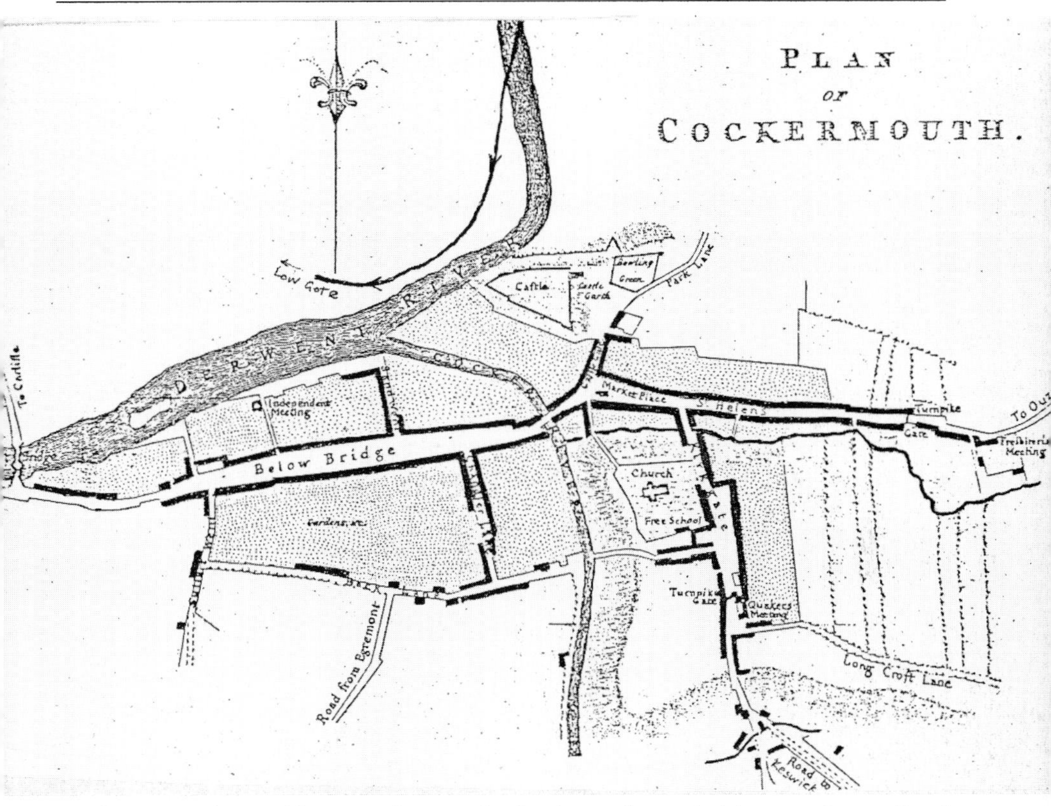

Hodkinson and Donald's map of 1775 clearly shows the typical layout of a medieval town – a wide main street with the burgage properties extending to Back Lane (later South Street) on the south and the river bank (later Waterloo Street) on the north. The heavy lines indicate the built-up street frontage and there has been considerable development since the map of 1620.

At the top of the map is Ladyboat weir on the Derwent from which a mill race runs south to curve westwards and eventually power the Gote mills. On the right is an indication of strip fields between St Helen's Street and Long Croft lane (now Windmill Lane). The Duke of Somerset had laid out his bowling green in the Castle Garth. The Moot Hall is shown in Market Place. Two of the town's turnpike gates are marked, both of which were moved further out as the town expanded – that in Kirkgate to near Rose Cottage and that in St Helen's Street to the Higham road corner. Tolls would be only a few years old in 1775. The 1711 church was the third on the site, to be burned down in 1850. The map shows the Independent/Congregational church temporarily split into the 'High Meeting' up St Helen's Street and the 'Low Meeting' off Below Bridge, the two to be reunited in 1782. What is now Wordsworth House, set back from the road opposite Sullart Street, had been built in 1745.

The map is of interest also for what it omits – no Station Street and Station Road in pre-railway days, no Castlegate Drive, only one school, no Christ Church before 1863 and no housing estates.

This 1919 postcard shows the confluence of the rivers as seen from the chimney of Derwent Mill. Left of the point is a tannery. At the left end of the bridge is Foundry House, with the windmill (two windows and partly in shadow) and foundry just beyond. To the right of All Saints church is the pyramidal roof of the Wesleyan Methodist church (now Town Hall/Tourist Office) and further right the rows of windows of Croft Mill.

The bridge, variously known as Waterloo, Brewery or Barrel Bridge, was washed away in the 1938 flood and replaced in 1963 by a footbridge – in the hope of preventing a recurrence, as it did not have a central pier for flood debris to lodge against. The angled building to the right was built as Wharton's linen mill in 1820. Waterloo Street runs to the lower right corner and there is much development between this and Main Street.

In contrast note the absence of housing estates on the edges of the town – beyond All Saints and in the Lorton Road area, just visible top right.

In 1901 Charles Bleasdale took this remarkable photograph of the town. The first feature one notices is the compactness of the town, almost completely confined between the River Derwent and South Street. In 1994 there are some twelve housing estates round the town centre. Bow-shaped Main Street, with the 1887 jubilee trees appearing like beads along both sides, goes up the centre. The Mayo statue and beyond it the Neddy clock can be seen. Top left a houseless Castlegate Drive above the castle is joined just off the picture by St Helen's Street which swings left top centre. Kirkgate (beyond the church spire) is built up, with Wordsworth Terrace and Fell View to the right and the Skinner Street area further right, on the edge of the photograph. Mitchell's Auction buildings and Fairfield schools are right of South Street and the workhouse buildings appear on the edge of the picture between Gallowbarrow and Sullart Street. Left of centre, the mill footbridge leads to Derwent Mill (Harris's linen at this time), just visible on the edge of the picture, with the race coming down from Ladyboat heading for the Gote mills. Derwent Bridge crosses the river bottom centre and the New Street estate, built 1856–7, is isolated bottom right. The single track railway from the Low Road goods yard (former terminus of the Cockermouth–Workington line) cuts across the bottom right corner to climb by a 1 in 70 gradient to the 1865 new station. Many individual buildings – churches, houses, mills, brewery, castle, etc. may be identified.

Cousin Charley's Day was the predecessor of the town's annual carnival – a procession with queens, bands and displays, followed by a gathering on Sandair sports field. Charles Bleasdale was editor of the *West Cumberland Times*. During the 1901 event he and a navigator went up in a balloon from Sandair, eventually landing near St Bees. This picture recalls the event and shows the great crowd on the cricket field, with Fitz Mill buildings in the background.

An aerial view of the Market Place and castle area which appeared in the press in 1982 and may be earlier than that date. The Derwent is visible top left, with some of Miller's buildings beyond, the Cocker curving to join it along the left-hand side. Left of centre are the brewery buildings. Right of centre is the castle, its elevated defensive position being clearly shown. The end of Market Place is bottom centre, Castlegate being lost between the buildings to the right. The full length of Banks Court is in the centre of the photograph.

SECTION TWO

Street Scenes

The tree-lined eastern end of Main Street with a very early Cumberland car registration.

Main Street a few years after the trees were planted to commemorate Queen Victoria's Jubilee in 1887. The roof line has not changed in a hundred years.

A light cart passing Wordsworth House, 1890s. Note that part of the surface is cobbled, also another Jubilee tree. Fletcher's ironmongery shop on the extreme right is now a bookshop and museum and was the office for obtaining fuel supplies during the last war. The blank wall with implements leaning against it was the harness room for Wordsworth House stables, now the National Trust shop.

A leisurely view in what is now the busiest part of Main Street, Croasdel's chemists shop being No. 64.

A delivery opposite the Appletree Hotel, 1890s. Note the substantial shop awning.

Everyone appears 'well muffled' in this view in snow near the 'Neddy' clock, 1890s. The Globe hotel is left of the clock.

Another Main Street view from the same point as the top picture. The cabby has the best view of the wedding. There is an interesting 1890s pram in the foreground.

The statue in Main Street is of Richard Southwell Bourke (1822–72), Earl Mayo. As Lord Naas he was an active and prominent politician who represented Cockermouth in Parliament for the period 1857–68 after serving as MP for constituencies in his native Ireland. In 1869 he was appointed Viceroy and Governor-General of India, where he was assassinated on 8 February 1872 when visiting a penal settlement. Three years later 'This Monument was erected to Commemorate the Services to his Country of LORD MAYO'.

In earlier times cars did not find it necessary to 'keep left'. Eventually the railings which protected Mayo and the corner lamps which protected motorists were removed. Disaster followed many years later.

Early one morning in 1964 a tanker crashed into the statue, demolishing the whole structure with the exception of the lowest block of the column. Surprisingly the driver survived.

Mayo suffered considerable damage, including decapitation. In a good light it is possible to see where he was put together again.

Restoration!

The monumental mason's yard in front of Walker Bros premises, part of their business. The building and the archway to the right remain unaltered.

These cottages were replaced by Cockermouth Library, one of many libraries in the country provided by the Carnegie trust, opened in 1904. The library moved here from rooms in the Savings Bank building (with clock tower) near Cocker Bridge. Walker Bros retained their access to the right of the picture.

Cockton's Yard was a housing development along burgage plots behind Nos 68 and 70 Main Street. Seen here in the early 1980s the property was empty and dilapidated, the right of way through the yard blocked by shrubs and willow herb. It was restored jointly by the North-west Building Preservation Trust (Civic Trust), the Department of the Environment, Allerdale District Council and Cumbria County Council at a cost of £240,000 and opened by Lord Montagu of Beaulieu, chairman of English Heritage, in March 1987.

Cockton's Yard when restoration was almost complete, before the appearance of trees, tubs of flowers and hanging baskets.

Main Street has always been well supplied with hotels and coffee houses. The Courtyard Café, shown here before its closure, occupied the yard and buildings behind No. 72, the premises first used by Robinson Mitchell for his auctions (see also p. 98).

Disused property along the west side of High Sand Lane in 1968, now replaced by flats. The portion with the large doors and gable was once a chair factory.

In the 1970s Nos 75–85 Main Street and property behind, leading into Strickett's Court, were empty and derelict. The council decided to restore the area, but before this was done archaeologists from Lancaster University carried out a rescue dig in 1980. Here two of the team are seen in action. Interesting discoveries were made, including the fact that the area was inhabitated at least as far back as 1300.

In 1988 Cockermouth endured the upheaval caused by the renewal of the town's Victorian sewerage system. Shafts were sunk at intervals along Main Street, as seen here, and connected by tunnels through which wagons ran. This method reduced considerably the disruption of traffic which would have been caused by opening up the whole length of the street.

Until 1965 the bottom end of Sullart Street was as narrow as the Kirkgate exit to Market Place. The road was widened by demolishing the back-to-back houses which were along the west side of the street and the Wordsworth Tavern on the Crown Street corner.

'Neddy' was erected as a memorial to Edward Waugh, MP for Cockermouth 1880–5. The clock had a bell to strike the hours, now in All Saints church. The plaque from the column is now on the front of the old Court House. Unfortunately 'Neddy' was not in the centre of Main Street, which led to its demolition in 1932 as a traffic hazard.

A view down Station Street with many interested children. On the extreme left is Sealby's shop, family grocers for a long period, and at the far end of the street is 'Neddy'.

The east side of Station Street once included the Public Hall, built in 1874–6 and the venue for meetings, lectures, dances, cinema shows, etc. It became unsafe and ceased to be used in the 1950s, finally giving place to the National Westminster Bank in 1974. Next to the hall is Brash Brothers shop behind which the *West Cumberland Times* was edited and printed before its amalgamation with the *Workington Star* in the 1970s. The editor Charles Bleasdale (Cousin Charley) is standing in the doorway wearing a dark suit.

A closer view of the Public Hall, which had a shop on each side of the entrance door, and the *Times* shop and office.

A carrier going to the station with a load from hotels or businesses in the town. Fairfield House is on the left and auction buildings and All Saints spire are in the background, but the Grand Theatre, built 1914, has not yet appeared. This card was posted on 22 December 1910.

An early sketch of Cocker Bridge looking towards Market Place. The low buildings on the left were replaced by the Savings Bank building with the clock tower.

Market Place from Cocker Bridge, from a card postmarked 1914. Huddart's shop on the left was demolished in the 1938 flood and the business moved into the premises next door. The third shop on the right would be Hird and Gate's grocery and general store (see also p. 44).

The Spread Eagle Inn yard, between Market Place and the brewery. The sign reads 'Spread Eagle Spirit Vaults'. An interesting feature was the public right of way of Brewery Lane which cut through a corner of the building – by the round archway in the corner. It was the birthplace of Thomas Cape who became MP for Cockermouth and Workington. The building has now been demolished.

A view of Market Place looking west, early this century. 'Red House' is on the extreme right and between the trees are the rounded door-heads of Cockermouth's first bank, the Carlisle City and District. The heavy metal door leading to steps down to the small strongroom still remains in the present shop.

Looking from All Saints churchyard across the clutter of buildings to the old hall, with the castle in the background, 1968. This area was cleared and the hall demolished in the early 1970s to form Bitter Beck car-park.

The rear of the south side of Market Place, 1973. The property to the left of the tall 'bacon house' was demolished, including the row of houses in Market Street just visible on the extreme left.

Bitter Beck flowing past the backs of houses and the ends of yards on the south side of St Helen's Street. The rows of property were shortened as part of the Bitter Beck Scheme of the 1970s and a grassed area was formed along the bank of the stream.

Kirkgate seen from All Saints steeple after the cemetery was made in the 1850s (the chapels and the curator's house are in the distance) and before the rebuilding of the Quaker Meeting House in 1884, the forecourt of which is beyond the gardens, with the large-roofed meeting house to its left. On the left is Little Mill on Tom Rudd Beck and the buildings on the extreme right are the almost enclosed square at the top of Kirkgate. Lorton Road stretches away into the distance.

Fletcher House, seen here in about 1930, stood at the corner of Kirkgate and Windmill Lane. It was demolished to widen the approach to the Windmill Lane housing estate. Holly Square, which still exists, is on the left, with the roof of the Quaker Meeting House behind.

In the 1940s and 1950s old railway wagons along Tweed Mill Lane served as offices for petrol companies that used a railway siding off the photograph to the right.

Brigham village looking east. The near group of houses on the left, the 'island site', was demolished in the late 1940s, leaving the present wide road junction.

A view of High Lorton village. The stepped houses and brewery building shown on p. 97 are right of centre, beyond the wall and trees.

SECTION THREE

Shops and Prices

Early guides to Cockermouth and district contain many advertisements. Only a few are reproduced here, mostly from Mate's Guide issued at the beginning of the century. Above is the Mayo Furnishing Warehouse of P. Robinson & Co., on the north side of Main Street near the statue. 'House Furnishers, Cabinet Makers, Decorators, Joiners and Undertakers' is the introduction to some thirty types of goods and services offered. 'By all means go to London to see the Sights but when you want Good Value in Furniture, Taste in Decoration and Good Workmanship, go to P. Robinson & Co.'

Johnston's café at 17 Station Street, 1920s.

Fisher and Co. in Station Street were 'Ironmongers, Plumbers, Bar, Iron and Steel Merchants, Gasfitters, Tin Plate Workers, Contractors, etc.'. The etc. included fireplaces, hearths, cutlery, electroplated goods and bedsteads. Fisher's sold the Improved Patent Cumberland Range and were sole agents for the Patent Peveril Stove.

Drummond's men's outfitters at 31 Station Street, *c.* 1900.

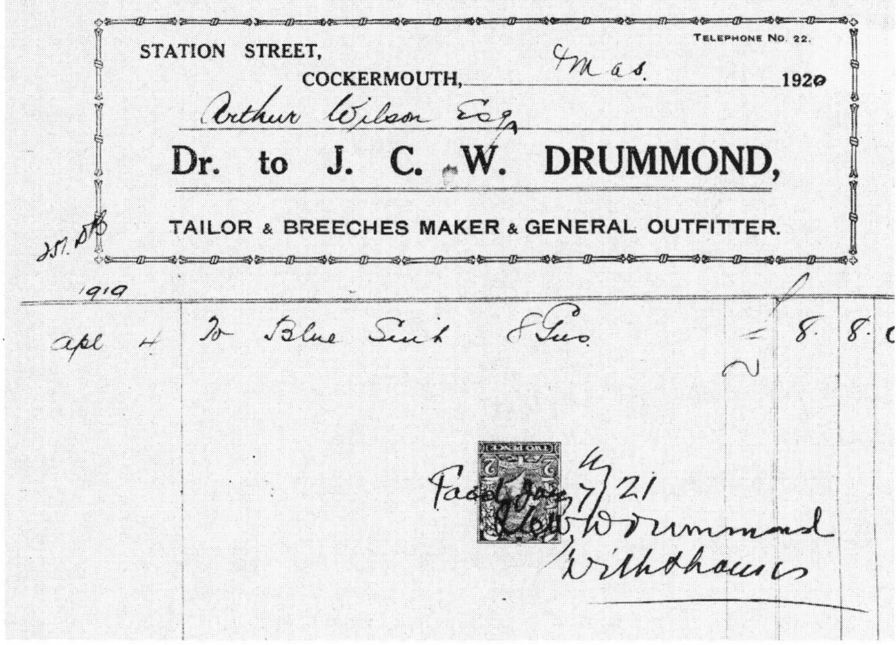

TELEPHONE No. 22.

STATION STREET,

COCKERMOUTH, 4 Mas. 1920

Arthur Wilson Esq.

Dr. to J. C. W. DRUMMOND,

TAILOR & BREECHES MAKER & GENERAL OUTFITTER.

1919					
apl 4	To Blue Suit & Trs		8.	8.	0

Paid Jan 7/21
J.C.W. Drummond
With thanks

£8 8*s* 0*d* was a lot of money in 1921, representing several weeks' wages for many workers.

Jonathan Cooper's drapery shop was a long-established business in Main Street.

Opposite Jonathan Cooper's was Josiah Hall's grocery shop, at No. 22. Like several Cockermouth shops it not only served the people of the town but through weekly visits of travelling vans supplied customers in many of the surrounding villages. Josiah's son Richard was the inspiration behind the opening of the youth hostel in Double Mills (see p. 126).

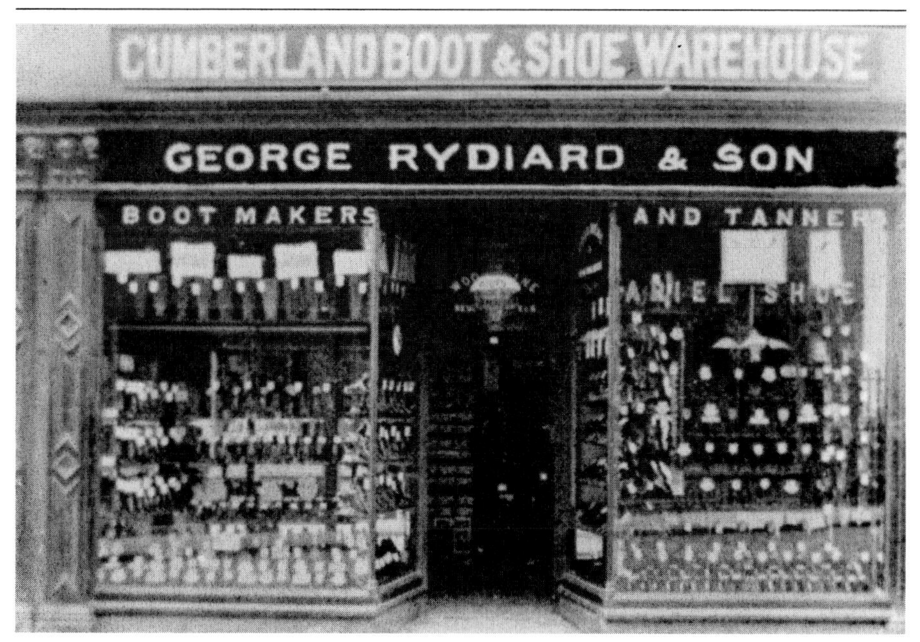

Mate's view of Rydiard's footwear shop by Cocker Bridge. The firm was renowned for its farm boots, made by their own craftsmen.

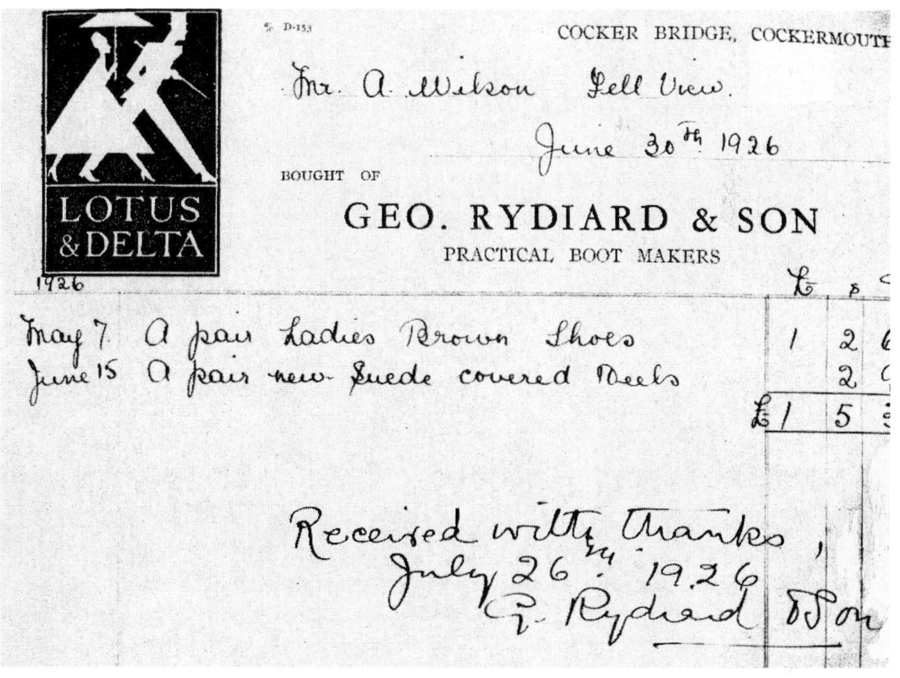

LOTUS & DELTA

1926

D-153

COCKER BRIDGE, COCKERMOUTH

Mr. A. Wilson Fell View.

June 30th 1926

BOUGHT OF

GEO. RYDIARD & SON

PRACTICAL BOOT MAKERS

		£	s	d
May 7.	A pair Ladies Brown Shoes	1	2	6
June 15	A pair new Suede covered Heels		2	
		£1	5	

Received with thanks, July 26th 1926 G. Rydiard & Son

Ladies' brown shoes cost £1 2*s* 6*d* a pair in 1926.

Mate's view of Huddart's shop by Cocker Bridge before it was undermined by flooding in 1938.

Banks shop faces up Market place. Seen here in 1900 it is still one of the town's two ironmongers. The premises have been flooded a number of times and the cellar has not been used since the 1938 flood. Even in earlier times security was a problem, for when closed the shop was protected by a sliding shutter which moved on a track running from the side of the shop and along the window base. A 'horse' was carried from the rear of the shop to block the doorway.

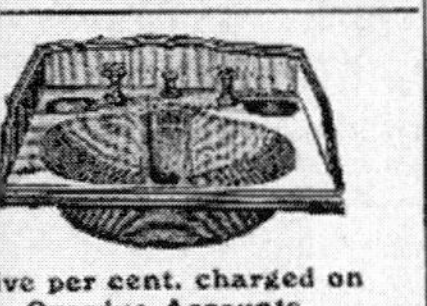

102, MAIN STREET, COCKERMOUTH.
October 1924

Mr A. Wilson

To HESKETT W. FLETCHER,

FURNISHING and GENERAL IRONMONGER,

REGISTERED PLUMBER,

Bell-Hanger, Gas-Fitter and Hot-Water Engineer.

STOVE and RANGE MANUFACTURER. TIN, IRON and ZINC PLATE WORKER.

Water Supplies, Cisterns. Water Closets, Baths. Lavatories and every description of Plumbers' Work fixed in the best manner.

ELECTRIC BELLS SUPPLIED AND FIXED.

SANITARY WORK EXECUTED WITH ALL THE LATEST IMPROVEMENTS.

ESTIMATES GIVEN.

Agent for the London and Provincial Fire Insurance Company.

A letterhead for the Fletcher firm in the premises, ~~now the National Trust shop,~~ described on p. 18.

6700

1897.

Mr WILSON

BEGS TO ANNOUNCE HER

ANNUAL SHOW

— OF —

French Fashions & Novelties

IN ALL DEPARTMENTS, COMMENCING

FRIDAY, APRIL 30th, 1897

84, MAIN STREET,
Cockermouth.

Ladies and Children's Millinery,
Laces, Veilings, Ribbons,
Flowers, Feathers, Gloves,
Sunshades, Mantles, Boleros,
Dress Materials, Silks, Velvets,
etc., etc.
Dressmaking in all its Branches.

Agent for Steam Laundry, Carlisle,
AND
Morton's, Dyers, Whitehaven.

AN INSPECTION RESPECTFULLY SOLICITED.

There were other clothes besides the shawls and aprons seen elsewhere in this book! Even isolated Cockermouth was not beyond French influence.

The Great Broughton branch of Hird & Gate grocers in Cockermouth (see also p. 31).

Cockermouth Corn Market

67244

Notice is hereby given to all whom it may Concern that on and after the 10th day of May 1897 the toll of one penny for every sack of wheat, Oats, barley rye, peas, or any other grain brought for the purpose of sale, or exposure for sale, into the Market of the Cockermouth Urban District Council will be strictly enforced in accordance with the published Table of Tolls -

John Fearon
Clerk to the Council

W C James
1 & 8 May
1897

This memo from the clerk to the council speaks for itself.

SECTION FOUR

River Scenes

The view north from Kirkbank, one of the best viewpoints in the town. The photograph was taken before the footbridge was erected in 1887. A ford then connected South Street with Cocker Lane; the building with the tall chimney in the foreground is No. 1 Cocker Lane. On the left bank of the river is Croft Mill, with the Midland Bank beyond at the end of Cocker Bridge. The long building right of the bridge is the hat factory, with the then Huddart's shop showing round the left-hand end. There are houses nearer on the river bank. The prominent building on the right, with the pyramid roof, is the Wesleyan Methodist Chapel (1841–1932). The castle stretches across the background.

A similar view to the last many years later, 1968. The hat factory still stands and the former chapel, now the Town Hall, is in need of painting. Left of the Town Hall and in the foreground are the shacks and shrubs which were cleared a few years later to make the present car park. Visible through the shrubs to the bottom left of the Town Hall is the long low building of the Hatters Arms, a light wall and one window showing.

The same view as above, *c.* 1980.

Cocker Bridge, *c.* 1980. The hat factory was replaced by Rydiard's shop (the large white gable) and the derelict houses between there and the archway were demolished.

The archway in the upper picture seen from the other side before the tidying up in the 1970s. The houses, later demolished, are on the right, backing on to the river, and their lavatories, etc., are on the left. The Town Hall is visible in the top left.

In the area shown in the last photograph is this small building, until recently the Tourist Information Centre but at one time the armoury of the Cockermouth branch of the Cumberland and Westmorland Yeomanry. Here they stored their weapons when not drilling. There are two barrel-vaulted rooms at ground level.

The confluence of the rivers, *c.* 1980. Brewery buildings are on the left, with the castle beyond, the windmill behind Foundry House, the footbridge of 1963 in the centre and the angled 1820 building of what was originally Wharton's linen mill on the right.

A placid view of Rubby Banks mills across the mill pool formed by the large dam on the right of the photograph. The culverts through which the water flowed to turn the two wheels inside the buildings are just hidden by the trees. On the right is a bridge leading to the mills' tenter fields, where the woven fabric was dried and stretched. At one time the bridge also led to the town's first golf course on the area, now an extension of Harris Park on that side of the river.

The river system affected the town in ways portrayed in the next few pages. Very severe floods were experienced when there was prolonged rain in the central fells. The Derwent reaches its peak in Cockermouth about two days before the Cocker and when these high levels overlap flooding is likely, though less so now water-power is no longer used, the weirs have collapsed and there is better river management. When in severe weather the rivers froze, the mill wheels stopped and much of the town's workforce was made idle, having to rely on help from their neighbours, as for example through the profits of the 'ice house' teas.

The worst floods in the town this century were in 1918, 1932 and 1938, but there were a number of lesser ones such as that in the Market Place area in 1966 caused by the collapse of a culvert following a storm east of the town. This 1932 view shows an isolated Mayo.

An opportunity being seized in Main Street outside the Huntsman Hotel.

Rising Station Street provides a dry footing from which to view a watery Main Street.

Cocker Bridge during the flood on August Bank Holiday, 1938, the river flowing through the basement of the Midland Bank into Main Street. Many Cockermouth records were ruined in the flooded bank strongrooms.

Brewery Bridge was badly damaged, 4 October 1918. In the upper view one of the rails has gone and debris is piled against the remaining one. By the time the lower photograph was taken this had also been breached. In spite of the damage the bridge, then of road width, was repaired.

These two views show the waterfall produced by debris building up against the central pier of the earlier Barrel, Brewery or Waterloo Bridge. The upper picture shows the tannery buildings along the Derwent bank, now a grassed area with seats. The lower view is towards High Sand Lane, 12 December 1932.

The last moments of Brewery Bridge, again including a rare record of the tannery, 1938.

Waterloo Street was particularly vulnerable to flooding, and is seen here with a castle tower in the background.

The Cocker taking a short cut down South Street, December 1932. The cottage No. 1 Cocker Lane is in the background, with the churchyard wall higher up. The water can be seen splashing over South Street or Quaker Bridge.

South Street leads to Challoner Street, seen here in the later flood of 1938, and so to Main Street.

Occasionally rivers freeze. The 'ice house' seen here was built from blocks cut from the frozen Cocker in 1895. The lower part of the photograph is the snow-covered river. It is reputed that tea was sold at the ice house, which stood for about eleven weeks, to raise money to help families whose incomes had ceased because of the stationary mill wheels.

Standing on the frozen Derwent at Ladyboat, up-river from the castle, January 1929. Mrs Mary Cook is second from the left.

SECTION FIVE

The Castle and other Homes

The Normans built the first castle in Cockermouth in the mid-twelfth century. The gatehouse shown here, which had a drawbridge, barbican, portcullis and three pairs of studded doors dates, from about 1400.

In the middle of last century Charles Wyndham, nephew of the lord of the manor General Henry Wyndham, made several drawings of the castle. This and the next five pictures are reproductions of his work.

The castle from the roadway. The absence of trees permitted a view no longer seen. Wyndham Row leads down to the left, the flag tower lives up to its name and the gatehouse is on the right.

Passing through the gatehouse and looking back from the outer bailey the 1847 family rooms are on the left, a home of the Dowager Lady Egremont; the caretaker's accommodation is beyond and to the right of the gatehouse are offices.

The outer bailey with the gatehouse entrance to the inner bailey still usable. Note that the gap between the 1805 family rooms and the kitchen tower has not yet been filled, leaving the windows of the mirk kirk (dark chapel) still unblocked.

An inner bailey view of the kitchen tower. The large arch was made last century to prevent further collapse of the wall in which it stands. The well is still in use and has not yet been fitted with the Victorian well-head and pump.

A north-west view of the castle with the Derwent in the foreground. Left to right: the outer gatehouse, family rooms, unfilled gap, kitchen tower, great hall, square bell tower in the background, late fourteenth-century family rooms, round tower.

Cockermouth Castle and the confluence of the rivers, a drawing by Nathaniel Buck dated 1739. The Cocker on the right is out of proportion and the building lines in the background are difficult to follow. The church is All Saints (1711–1850).

Branthwaite Hall was used for some years as the headquarters of opencast coal mining in West Cumbria. This necessitated considerable restoration of the former farm house. The photograph shows the fourteenth-century peel tower and the 1604 wing beyond it – with some modern touches at road level.

Isel Hall is seen here across the Derwent, the sixteenth-century range of buildings almost hiding the earlier peel tower behind.

The drawing room in Wordsworth House. Built by the sheriff of Cumberland in 1745 it was the birthplace of William and Dorothy Wordsworth whose father was agent for the Lowther property in the area and consequently allowed to live in the house. Rescued by the townspeople from demolition to make way for a bus station, it was handed to the National Trust in October 1938.

The old hall immediately before demolition in 1973, seen from the small yard on the Market Place side. Notice the blocked windows of what was once an attractive Elizabethan house. The plaque on the wall now stands on a column in the car park and reads – 'On the 17th. May 1568 there came to this house as a guest of Henry Fletcher, Esq., Mary Queen of Scots on her journey from Workington to Carlisle' – not quite correct as the hall was probably mostly rebuilt soon after her visit.

After the Fletcher family left the hall it was divided into tenements, with an inn at one end. It was cleared of occupants under a slum clearance scheme in 1937 and demolished in 1973. In the foreground of this picture a garden once extended to the churchyard wall, with an open stream flowing through it.

A view of the hall was opened up by the demolition in the early 1970s of sheds on what had once been the garden. Efforts were made to save the building but deterioration had gone too far. The photograph shows blocked and altered windows and even floor levels had been changed inside.

Fletcher Christian, who was to become famous as leader of the mutiny on the *Bounty*, was born at Moorland Close in 1764. The farm, between Cockermouth and Eaglesfield, is enclosed by a defensive wall, the gateway shown in the view below having strong doors. The lower view shows the farm *c.* 1900.

A commemorative plaque on Moorland Close farm.

The plaque on John Dalton's birthplace in Eaglesfield. Dalton was a member of a Quaker family and attended the school in Pardshaw Meeting House (see also p. 77). He spent most of his life in Manchester and rose to a position of renown in academic and scientific circles, being remembered primarily for his work on atomic structure.

Higham Hall in the early 1950s when a youth hostel.

Brigham Hall which stood by the main street. It was demolished early this century.

SECTION SIX

Churches and Schools

Brigham church, centre of a parish which extended from the Marron to Bassenthwaite Lake. All Saints, Cockermouth, was one of several chapels of ease under this mother church. The building, developed in the eleventh to fourteenth centuries, has nineteenth-century restorations and contains remains of pre-Norman crosses.

In 1930 a garden party at All Saints vicarage was part of the celebrations of Canon Parker's Jubilee. The Bishop presided.

Dean church dates from the twelfth century, with chancel and sanctuary additions in the fifteenth and seventeenth centuries. The base of a preaching cross, of the twelfth century or earlier, is on the left.

Wythop old church, pictured here, was demolished and replaced by the present St Margaret's, on the other side of the hill, in 1864. A few stones remain and an annual service is held on the site.

Most of Bridekirk's Norman church was used in the construction of the 'modern' church in 1868–70. The 1870 church is famous for its richly carved twelfth-century font, presenting a mixture of Scandinavian Runes and English Christianity. Presumably this once stood in the earlier church shown here.

The Wesleyan Methodist church (1841–1932), later the Town Hall and then the Tourist Information Centre, photographed *c.* 1900.

The church above had a popular non-conformist design – a square building with ground floor, gallery with the organ at the front, the pulpit between the two levels and a basement Sunday School.

The gallery level in the Methodist church.

The interior of the church at a harvest festival, the organ at the top and the pulpit in the centre of the 1890s photograph. The outline of the gallery and the supporting pillars are still visible in the present Tourist Information Centre.

A concert in the church basement, which in later Town Hall days became a popular venue for jumble sales, dancing classes, first aid instruction, etc.

A celebration tea in the forecourt of the Methodist church. In the 1890s there was apparently a path leading from the gate to the church door, bordered by lawns.

In 1932, the year of Methodist union, the Wesleyan Methodists left their 1841 building for new premises in Lorton Street. We see here a group on the church steps at the opening on 16 April. Front row, left to right: Mr Robinson, Mr Mossop Fox, -?-, Revd C. Smith, Miss Agnew,-?-, -?-. Remainder, left to right: Mr H. Harry Vickers, Mr Marwell, Mrs G. Sealby, Mr T. Birkett, Mr J. Cook, Mr Gill, Mr Nelson, -?-, Mr Howarth, Revd Mr Price, Mr Clulow, Mr Mann, Mr J. Collins.

The spring synod of the Carlisle District of the Methodist church met in Cockermouth in 1978. From the left are Revd John Hinds (URC), Revd John Crawley (Rector of All Saints), Revd Ronald H. Brown (Chairman of the District), Revd J. Michael Taylor (Methodist), Mr Leslie Cleeland (Mayor), -?-, and Revd Brian White (Methodist).

Behind the 1850 United Reformed church stands the earlier Independent/Congregational church building, now converted to community residential accommodation. The photograph shows the attractive porch and the datestone of 1719, happily retained in the conversion.

The conversion of the 1719 building was made possible by dividing the church horizontally in 1990, with the church upstairs, as pictured, and other accommodation on the ground floor.

The church of St Michael and All Angels in Isel dates from about 1130 on a pre-Norman site. Left of the two-light fifteenth-century chancel window (near the centre of the picture) are small incised dials on the door jamb. Among early fragments of sculpture was the triskele stone, with designs carved on each of four faces, including the 'triskele' (three-limbed symbol) shown here. It dated from about AD 900 and was stolen from the church in 1986.

In Eaglesfield there was a Quaker burial ground by 1670 and in 1711 the meeting house shown here was built for use only at funerals. For a period it also served as the village hall and a cooking range was installed for use in evening classes. It was converted into a house about 1980. This sketch appeared in Margaret Irwin's book on Pardshaw Meeting written in 1918.

Over the entrance to the above meeting house is the inscription 'John Barn gave 40££ to build this house 1711'.

The Friends Meeting House and burial ground at Pardshaw Hall seen from low on the Crags in 1918. The main building, behind the row of four trees, was erected in 1729 to succeed a lean-to building against a limestone outcrop on the Crags. On the extreme right are the stables and schoolroom, the former having incorporated in it the 1672 datestone from the Crags.

Last century a sword made in about 50 BC was found in Wythop. It is now in the British Museum and in 1985 a replica was made for Embleton church by two apprentices at British Steel. In front the apprentices, Michael Wright and Anthony Rae, hold the sword and Revd Colin Fuller is on the right. A fairly modern picture to commemorate one of the two oldest features mentioned in this book.

The Free School of Cockermouth and Embleton building, erected in 1676 to house a school that had probably been founded in the previous century. This is as it appeared in the 1890s, shortly before its demolition and replacement by All Saints church rooms.

The end view of the old grammar school which counted Fletcher Christian and a very young William Wordsworth among its pupils. It had a wide curriculum and built up a good reputation, but dilapidation of the building became a problem in its later years.

The Industrial School seen from the Lorton Road/Strawberry How corner before the trees grew. It was opened in 1881 for boys referred for vagrancy or crime by courts in Cumberland county and closed in 1921. Cockermouth Secondary School was opened in the premises in 1929, later becoming Cockermouth Grammar School.

The Grammar School from the back in about 1980.

Boys in the Industrial School were taught a trade and these two pictures, taken for a prize day sheet of photographs in 1910, show the joiners' shop and the shoemakers' shop. Other possibilities were tailoring and cookery.

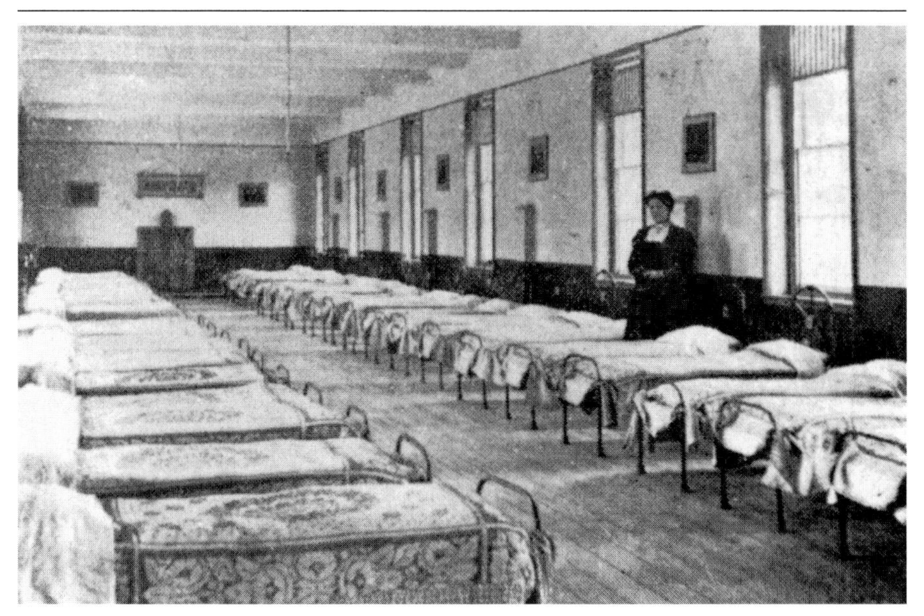

A dormitory in the Industrial School, 1907. Twenty years later it was divided into classrooms for the secondary school.

A picture of the boys drilling, 1907. The school was famous for its band which played on civic occasions. It had a roll of over a hundred.

The Grammar School staff, 1947–8. Back row, left to right: Miss A.M. Mackenzie, T.B. Ferguson, N.T. Brown, J.B. Bradbury, T.M. Harris, R. Ross, Mrs Richardson (secretary) Middle row: Miss M.D. Shackleton, Mrs S. Clarke, C. Birtwistle, Mrs M. Southgate, Miss E.M. Sinclair, Miss M. Wilkinson, J.C. Southgate, Miss W.D. Whitehead, Mrs J.V. McLeish, Miss E. Ray. Front row: Miss V. Stoddart, Miss J.I. Sewell, Miss C.L. Maclennan, Miss O. Simpson (senior mistress), W.R. Booth (headmaster), E.E. Bacon, R. James, D. Rigby, A.G. Barnes.

SECTION SEVEN

Industry

An early view of the confluence of the rivers. There are tannery buildings along the Derwent bank on the left, with a house and drying washing on the extreme left. There is no bridge across the Cocker outlet, so the view is before 1887. There is no Foundry House but more tannery buildings and early brewery premises up the narrow Cocker. Two culverted sections of the race which powered the two mills in Waterloo Street are seen on the right but are apparently out of use by this time.

The two Low Gote mills in 1968. The race ran from the bottom right corner and was split into two, one flow powering the wheel shown and the other turning a wheel on the gable end of the further building.

The Papcastle road side of the two Low Gote mills with the Maryport pump house chimney beyond.

The Low Gote area, 1968. The flax drying building (see also p. 88) is front centre and the two Low Gote mills are just visible behind it to the left. The chimney is that of the Maryport water pumping station.

Postmarked 1908, this card shows the extensive Fitz mill complex seen across the mill weir on the Derwent. The weir had a fish pass. Owned by the Senhouses of the Fitz, it produced a variety of goods over the years but was marked 'disused' on the 1910 map. It is now demolished.

The chimney of the water pumping station serving Maryport was demolished in March 1974, prior to the conversion of the pump house into residential accommodation. It was an attractive square, stepped erection, 110 ft high. The building is on the road to Papcastle from the foot of Gote Brow. Water was pumped from a well, not from the Derwent which flows alongside.

Harold Wilson performed the official opening of James Walker and Co.'s seals, gaskets and packaging factory, built in 1969. With him are Mr A. Gibbs, managing director (left), and Mr R.W. Strong, executive chairman.

A postcard of Derwent Mill, 1915. The main buildings were erected by Messrs Harris in 1834, 1847 and 1855. This linen firm closed down in the early 1930s and Millers Footwear came from Great Yarmouth early in the war and stayed until closure in July 1990. The footbridge on the right was provided as a short cut for the mill employees but gradually became a public right of way. The site and larger buildings are being converted to other uses.

On 7 November 1992 Fred Dibnah demolished the unwanted chimney of Derwent Mill. It had been a Cockermouth landmark for a century and a half.

The Harris firm began manufacturing in one of the Low Gote mills before building Derwent Mill in 1834 and they erected this flax-drying building in adjacent Spittle Ings. The openings were slatted, not glazed, to allow ventilation. Sometimes referred to as 'the hospice' because somewhere here was a hospice run by the Black Friars for travellers crossing the Derwent (Spittle Ings = hospital meadows), it is now a house.

J. HARRIS
& SONS, LTD.

DERWENT MILLS
COCKERMOUTH

Jonathan Harris & Sons, Limited,
LINEN and LINEN THREAD
MANUFACTURERS,
ART NEEDLEWORK DESIGNERS,
TRACERS and EMBROIDERERS.

Head Office, Studios, and Works—
Derwent Mills, Cockermouth.

LONDON—
Wholesale only—50 Bow Lane, E.C. 4.
West End Showrooms—91 Wigmore Street, W. 1.
BIRMINGHAM—4 Midland Arcade, New Street.
GLASGOW—134 Mains Street, Sauchiehall Street.
(Four Doors from Sauchiehall Street).
LIVERPOOL—
Miss Florence M. Barnes, 47 Bold Street.
MANCHESTER—33 King Street.

Coming from Ireland early last century, Harris soon became a well-known name. The firm was famous for its 200 shades of embroidery threads and had showrooms in major cities and in Paris.

There was a corn mill on the Double Mills site as early as 1478. Here we see a sluice gate open in one of the two races which powered the wheels, returning water to the Cocker in the foreground.

Double Mills became disused and was bought by the Urban District Council. A number of uses were considered and in 1933 it was leased to the Youth Hostel Association. It stands in a curve of the River Cocker, which may be seen in the background. Leaning against the bank on the right is a French burr millstone.

An up-river view of the two Rubby Banks mills, 1968 (see also p. 49). The buildings were demolished about 1970.

Rubby Banks mills usually produced textiles, but there were short periods of other uses. For some years in the 1950s and 1960s Oswald Hartley did wood-turning in one of the buildings, using water power to produce electricity to turn the shafting. Here we see a belt drive to a lathe, Mr Hartley standing alongside. The frames of two tables with turned legs are in the centre.

Another variation from the usual textiles was the use of Rubby Banks by William Smethurst, born in Salford in 1813, for his business of hatter and furrier.

This letter heading used by William Smethurst is an interesting up-stream view of Rubby Banks in the nineteenth century showing the two mills. The river flows to the left of the complex and the exits of the two races which have powered the wheels inside the buildings are clearly seen. The mill house is to the right, with a workshop and store (now also a house) beyond.

This view down the river to Cocker Bridge was apparently recorded before the present Midland Bank building was erected and when Croft Mill (left) had a chimney. Beyond the right-hand end of the bridge is the shop demolished following the 1938 flood. The long building on the right is the hat factory, with houses on the river bank in front. The round arch is the exit of Bitter Beck into the Cocker. There are glimpses of brewery buildings and of the castle in the background.

Croft Mill before conversion into flats, 1970. A textile mill for most of its existence it occasionally changed to hats and is now known, rather misleadingly, as 'Hatters Croft'.

The Tweed Mill, erected in 1872–4 with the latest equipment for lighting, heating and machine power, was never a success. It accommodated every process in the manufacture of tweed, but employees were being dismissed by 1877 and it was sold in 1883. Subsequently used by another textile firm, a confectionery business, a car manufacturer, etc., the mill and its landmark chimney were eventually demolished, leaving a few outbuildings and the name Tweed Mill Lane.

An opening in the bottom corner of Kirkgate Square led to one of Cockermouth's two rope-walks, seen here derelict in 1968. The essentials were a long piece of land and a warehouse, both seen here but with a later greenhouse intruding. The town's other rope-walk was behind the west side of Station Street, now the rear approach to the shops.

Cockermouth had two windmills. Of one only the name Windmill Lane remains. The other still stands, surprisingly situated on the banks of the two rivers at their confluence. It probably ground bark for use in the pits of the two neighbouring tanneries.

The earlier Brewery Bridge with a central pier. Beyond are tannery buildings on the left, Foundry House in the centre and the foundry with chimney on the right.

Armstrong was a timber merchant with premises occupying much of the centre of the town. The offices shown lined the north side of South Street until cleared for Walter Willson's car park. The chimney was erected in about 1860 for a steam engine and from 1914 was used as a ventilator for a Tangye gas engine.

Founded *c.* 1800, Armstrong's business diversified, as shown in this 1860 advertisement. The dynamite mentioned was stored in a shed at the end of the row of Sawmill Cottages, workers' accommodation on the site! The firm pioneered the clinicon block house during the brick shortage in the early 1950s. There are now a number of subsidiary companies – timber, transport, housing, etc. Timber activities were transferred to Flimby in the 1980s.

A team of Armstrong's own horses hauling timber on the outskirts of Cockermouth.

A load of timber from the country arriving at the Main Street entrance to Armstrong's timber yard in the last century.

Beyond these stepped houses in High Lorton can be seen the building (now a house) in which Jennings Bros, the Cockermouth brewers, began their business.

A brewery steam lorry, a product of the neighbouring foundry of Herbert Brothers.

No. 72 Main Street was the first site of the auction business begun by Robinson Mitchell in about 1850. He moved to Fairfield in 1860. This gallery, reached by steps from bottom right, was the place from which the auctioneer conducted the sale of horses in the yard below.

The warehouse facing the auctioneer's gallery shown above. Used by J.W. Mounsey, grocer, until 1980, it became a restaurant, the Courtyard Café.

SECTION EIGHT

The Railway

The first railway in the town linked Cockermouth with Workington in 1847. The terminus was on Low Road until 1865 when a connection with the new Cockermouth–Keswick–Penrith line and the new station was made by a single track which crossed the arches in the background. Some remnants of the first station remained until recently and are seen here in 1968.

Gallowbarrow footbridge which crossed the connecting line a short distance west of Cockermouth station.

A train entering Cockermouth station on the Up line. There were extensive cattle pens on the other side of the cattle wagons seen here.

This postcard of passengers waiting on the Up platform has a postmark of 1911.

The West Cumberland section of the Lakes Express standing in Cockermouth station shortly before the line closed in 1966. It was joined at Oxenholme by the other half from Windermere and ran to Euston as a through train. The journey from Cockermouth took about nine hours.

Looking down the Cocker when the railway viaduct was being constructed for the opening of the Cockermouth–Keswick–Penrith line in 1865. Under the right-hand arch may be seen the Wesleyan Methodist chapel (later the Town Hall and the Tourist Information Centre).

On the viaduct during construction. Some permanent way has been laid, but there are still contractor's tracks. The hill to the left became Harris Park. The workhouse buildings which stood on the site of the present Fairfield View and Fitz View flats are visible top right.

A train crossing the original rounded bridge over the Cocker, replaced by the present rectangular arches in the mid-1940s.

A Penrith-bound train in Bassenthwaite Lake station. Diesel units were introduced on 3 January 1955.

A steam-headed excursion in Cockermouth. The line to the right of the island platform was the terminus for Maryport trains, which ran via the Derwent branch line of the Maryport–Carlisle Railway, reversing at Brigham and Bullgill.

Brigham station, junction for the Derwent branch, closed in 1966 and the site is now under the A66 road.

The station from the park in the 1890s. Note the refreshment room on the right.

A rival to the railways – one of two AEC buses which ran the Harrington to Maryport service from 1925.

A variety of transport outside the Pheasant Inn at Dubwath.

Another threat to the railways. A pilot touring the country with a light aircraft gave flights from Park House field, near the hospital. In this photograph Norah Quail, a member of the Rydiard family, is in the centre.

SECTION NINE

Celebrations and Celebrities

Queen Victoria's Diamond Jubilee in 1897 was the inspiration for this commemorative arch in Crown Street. The gateposts of Grecian Villa are on the left, the doctor's house (now the Trout Hotel) in shadow on the right.

Edward, Prince of Wales, visited West Cumberland in 1927. He is seen here in Cockermouth, on the extreme right.

Princess Alexandra opened the swimming pool in May 1978, the result of years of fund raising and planning by the people of Cockermouth.

The Waterloo, Brewery or Barrel footbridge was opened in 1963, a long time after the destruction of the original road bridge by the 1938 flood. Seen at the opening are, left to right: Councillor M. Oglethorpe, Mr John E. Roanwood, Councillor G. Rook and Mr Joseph Mounsey.

A tree was planted by the mayor, Stephen Coates, and the mayoress, Claire Craig, to celebrate the move in 1987 of the town clinic from Harford House in Crown Street to purpose-built premises in the hospital campus.

THE NATIONAL TRUST

request the pleasure of the Company of

Misses D & E. Goodale

at the Opening of

WORDSWORTH HOUSE
COCKERMOUTH

on SATURDAY, JUNE 3rd, 1939, at 3 o'clock

By E. de Selincourt, Esq., D.Litt., F.B.A.,
(formerly Professor of Poetry in the University of Oxford).

Mrs. W. S. Dickson, on behalf of the National Trust, will receive the Deeds of the Property from J. W. Limon, Esq., J.P.

R.S.V.P. to
B. L. Thompson, Esq.
Troutbeck,
Windermere.

As mentioned elsewhere (p. 62) the town rescued Wordsworth House from demolition by raising £1,625 to buy it and £900 for repairs. This is an invitation from its new owners to the official opening in 1939.

In 1978 Cockermouth Rotary, Round Table and Lions groups combined to erect a bust of William Wordsworth opposite Wordsworth House to commemorate the bicentenary of the poet's birth. In 1986 the Round Table, with the help of local people and the Manpower Service Commission, landscaped the surrounding area. Here it is being 'opened' by the mayor, Stan Mercer, and mayoress, Pauline Wilson (left front). Jack Abernethy, chairman of Round Table, is in front of the bust.

In 1970 nearly 30,000 daffodil bulbs were planted on roadside verges in Cockermouth to celebrate the bicentenary of William Wordsworth's birth. School pupils assisted in the planting and here Fairfield Junior School children are seen in action.

Planting daffodils on the old Belle Vue roundabout under the direction of parks superintendent Mr Pitts.

In the summer of 1981 Dale Campbell-Savours, MP, planted a whitebeam in Harris Park on behalf of the Cockermouth Peace Group, marking the anniversary of the atomic bombing of Hiroshima and Nagasaki. He is seen here in action, assisted by the rector, Revd John Crawley.

A recent photograph included to record Cockermouth's very active twinning with Marvejols in France. Here the mayor Margaret Jackson plants a twinning tree in the Memorial Gardens.

Princess Anne at the opening on 30 March 1987 of the Cumbria Fire Service Headquarters on the site of the former railway station.

A modern photograph of an historic event shows the Princess Royal unveiling a plaque on the new Scout Centre in June 1991, watched by Charles Crane, chairman of the Centre Project Group.

In 1893 the widow of Joseph Harris, of the Derwent Mill linen firm, offered the town £2,000 to purchase land for a park in his memory. Thirteen acres on Rubby Banks were bought and here we see the official opening in 1895 of Harris Park.

A drinking fountain, a memorial to William and Dorothy Wordsworth, was unveiled in Harris Park. The ceremony was male dominated!

SECTION TEN

Leisure Activities

Under statutes of the sixteenth century, farm workers, male and female, had to attend a 'hiring fair' in the nearest market town to find employment for the next six months. To aid farmers in choosing employees those seeking employment carried a symbol of their speciality – carter's whipcord, blacksmith's hammer, shepherd's crook, cow hair for a cowherd or dairymaid, etc. The workers on their part were looking for 'a good meat shop', for they were to live with the farm family for six months once a bargain was sealed. Here we see the men's fair in 1929 at the Cocker Bridge end of Market Place, the women and girls by this time having moved to their own site in the Market Hall. 'Hiring' dwindled during the Second World War and in this form ceased altogether in Cockermouth about 1950.

The hiring fairs provided a variety of entertainment for many who possibly only left their farms and villages on these two occasions a year. They would have their wages to spend and there was much rowdyism and drunkenness. Now only the amusement element remains, at the spring holiday and at Martinmas in November.

Fair preparations, 1890s. The Globe Hotel is on the right.

Fairgoers were attracted into tents to see a wide variety of 'entertainment' – Russia's outsize giantess, a boy far gone with consumption, etc. Here we have a healthier entertainment by acrobats. The shop of Clementson, plumber and gasfitter, can be seen behind.

Large roundabouts in the wider part of Main Street during a fair, 1890s.

The smaller stalls were at the Cocker Bridge end of Main Street and in Market Place. This photograph of the Whitsun Fair in 1968 was taken from a window of Rydiard's shoe shop.

The procession on Cousin Charley's Day (predecessor of Cockermouth Carnival) passing through Market Place, *c.* 1900. The banner reads 'West Cumberland Times. Success to Cousin Charley's Children's Day'.

The Cousin Charley's Day procession passing Wordsworth House on the way to Sandair.

In the first half of this century many productions were staged in the Grand Theatre, with Cockermouth actors and a Cockermouth orchestra. Here we see the cast of *The Pirates of Penzance*, which ran from 4 to 7 May 1921.

Cockermouth Territorials marching along St Helen's Street, a picture included here because membership was a part-time activity.

An 1890s record of a dancing bear which toured the towns and villages, seen here outside the Huntsman Hotel.

It was usual for a circus to parade through the town to advertise its arrival and to encourage custom. This may be Sanger's Circus.

Cockermouth Civic Society (later Trust) was formed in 1967. Here we see members at an art and craft exhibition, *c.* 1970. Left to right: Mrs N. Quayle, Mr C. Elliott, Mrs D. Mason, Miss E. Goodlad, Mrs A. Goodlad, Mr S.M. Hamer, Mr D. Sekers, Mr R. Dickenson.

Over the years the Civic Trust has organized a number of litter sweeps in the town. Here a young group take advantage of a low river in 1976 to do some tidying up of the Cocker near Jubilee Bridge. Their haul included several panels of a car and a length of heavy hose used on petrol tankers. Left to right: Susan Ashworth, -?-, Catherine Bradbury, Margaret Bradbury, Christine Hodgson and Carol Hodgson.

The otter hounds passing under Jubilee Bridge.

Hounds meet at the Pheasant Inn, Piel Wyke (Bassenthwaite Lake).

Cockermouth Cycle Club, *c.* 1900.

W.H. Youdale was a draper in the town and also an accomplished photographer to whose skill we are indebted for many of the pictures in this volume. He is seen here in a car with an early Cumberland registration.

Twenty-four odd craft negotiating the rapids formed by the remains of Rubby Banks weir, part of a mile-long raft race on the rivers Cocker and Derwent. The mills in the background were demolished in 1971.

Cockermouth children (and adults!) watch a Punch and Judy show in Main Street before the switching-on of the 1986 Christmas lights by David Essex, an event attended by more than 10,000 people.

Like the territorials, membership of the fire brigade was a part-time voluntary occupation. Cockermouth brigade is seen here on Fairfield, with cattle auction buildings behind. Note the 1890s motive power.

Early market towns were self-supporting in food, textiles, leather, wooden articles, ropes, a wide variety of metal goods, etc. Cockermouth was no exception and the chest shown here was made and carved by Harry Peil in his workshop in the town. Industry, leisure activity, or both?

Higham Hall was built *c.* 1800 and was for seventy-six years the home of the Hoskins family. We see it here in the 1890s. The Fisher family moved in early this century. In 1951 it opened as a youth hostel (see also p. 66) and three years later became a residential school for girls until 1974. Later a centre for further education, it is now the successful Lake District Adult Education College.

Double Mills (see also p. 89) had ceased to grind corn by 1900 and eventually the Urban District Council bought it. Through the enthusiasm of Richard Hall, a member of a Main Street grocery firm, in 1933 the premises were leased from the council and opened as a youth hostel. Here we see people making their way to the official opening on 13 April, one of them being E. St J. Catchpool, national secretary of the YHA.

This final picture records earlier times than any other in this book. In 1984 houses were built in the grounds of the Burroughs, a large Papcastle house, which involved demolishing the gardener's cottage and clearing the orchard. The site being in the civil settlement area of the Roman camp of Derventio, a rescue dig was first undertaken by the Cumbria and Lancashire archaeology unit, based at Lancaster University. Here Adrian Olivier, in charge of the dig, and the author stand among the remains of Roman buildings.

Acknowledgements

This book would not have been possible without the contributions of many people who enabled me to collect and present in a suitable form over 200 black and white photographs of Cockermouth.

In the 1890s, as mentioned in the introduction, W.H. Youdale produced 100 slides of Cockermouth and the photographs of the hiring fair in 1850 and the building of the railway viaduct in the 1860s are also his.

Cockermouth Civic Society was formed in 1967 and one of their first activities was to commission two members, Mr Kelt and Mr J.W. Mounsey, to make a photographic record of the town. I have used much of their work, which is dated 1968.

Many of the street scenes of early this century are from postcards produced by the firms mentioned in the introduction. There was much duplication and I have made a selection of their work. I am indebted to more recent professionals for granting me permission to use copyright material – Ivor Nicholas, P.W. Robinson and R. Sankey. I have failed to trace R. Bonnington and M.I.B. Radcliffe who are no longer in this area, and Studio 18 once in Workington. If they see this book I hope they will contact me. I am greatly indebted to the Cockermouth people, too many to list, who over the years have given or loaned photographs, and hope they will accept this collective 'thank you'.

I owe much to the photographic staff of the *West Cumberland Times and Star* for searching their records and providing me with copyright prints. I am also greatly indebted to Harold Burslem, Cockermouth photographer, who made many reproducable prints from some very unpromising material. Finally my thanks to the staff of Alan Sutton Publishing, in particular Simon Fletcher and Lucy Stringer, for dealing with my many telephone calls and enabling this book to come to fruition.